DWIGHT DAVID EISENHOWER

DWIGHT DAVID EISENHOWER

SOLDIER AND STATESMAN

BY WILLIAM JAY JACOBS

A First Book
Franklin Watts
New York / Chicago / London / Toronto / Sydney

Cover art by Jane Sterrett

Photographs copyright ©: Dwight D. Eisenhower Library: pp. 2, 8, 12, 14, 15, 17, 20, 23, 24, 27, 29, 30, 35, 38 (both U.S. Army), 37 (Pace), 41 (Press Photographers Association of N.Y.), 43, 44, 53 (both National Park Service), 48, 50, 55 (all U.S. Navy); U.S. Army Photograph: p. 33.

Library of Congress Cataloging-in-Publication Data
Jacobs, William Jay.
    Dwight David Eisenhower / by William Jay Jacobs.
        p. cm. — (A First Book)
        Includes bibliographical references and index.
        ISBN 0-531-20191-0
        1. Eisenhower, Dwight D. (Dwight David), 1890–1969—Juvenile litera-
ture. 2. Presidents—United States—Biography—Juvenile literature. 3.
Generals—United States—Biography—Juvenile literature. 4. United States.
Army—Biography—Juvenile literature. [1. Eisenhower, Dwight D. (Dwight
David), 1890–1969. 2. Presidents. 3. Generals.] I. Title. II. Series.
E836.J28 1995
973.921'092—dc20
[B]
                                        94-22494
                                          CIP
                                          AC

CONTENTS

*People of Western Europe. A landing was
made this morning on the coast of France by
troops of the Allied Expeditionary Force. . . .
I call upon all who love freedom to stand with
us now. Together we shall achieve victory.*

—Dwight David Eisenhower
Broadcast on D-Day, June 6, 1944

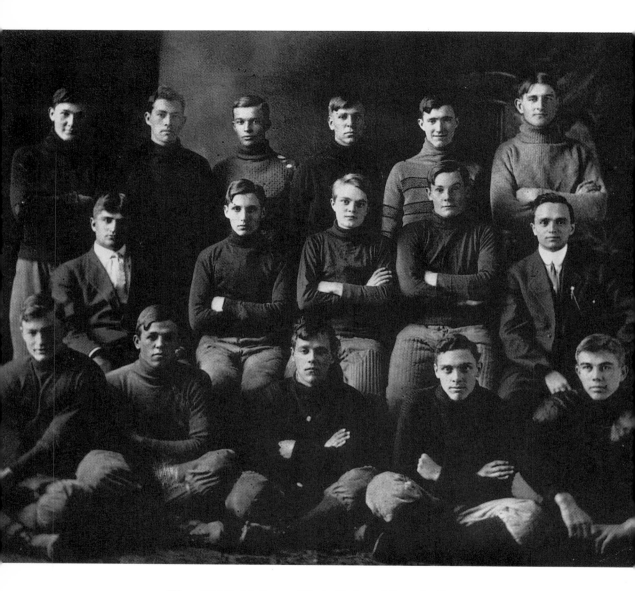

The 1909 Abilene High School football team;
Dwight is third from the left in the last row

A CRITICAL INCIDENT

"**G**uard the door, Edgar!" said Dwight. "And if they try to amputate my leg, stop them. I'd rather die than live with only one leg."

It all had begun with a race along a wooden platform, some good-natured shoving, and then a fall. At first, the fifteen-year-old Dwight Eisenhower thought nothing of the raw, exposed wound on his knee. As a star of the Abilene (Kansas) High School football team he was used to injuries.

In fact, he actually enjoyed the jarring contact of a hard tackle or of driving ahead, plunging into the line to gain an extra yard after being hit. Nor, as a boxer, did he mind taking a punch in order to deliver one of his own.

This time, though, the pain had not gone away. Instead it had gotten worse. Soon, ugly blue and red streaks appeared around the wound.

Blood poisoning!

All night long Dwight's mother stayed by his bedside. Every day, three times a day, a doctor came to the house, applying the only medicines he had—rubbing alcohol and generous doses of carbolic acid—causing Dwight to scream with pain.

But nothing seemed to help. As the poison spread upward, Dwight became delirious with fever, not even knowing where he was or who he was.

"We have to operate," said the doctor finally. "In another day it will be too late."

"Remember your promise," Dwight told his older brother Edgar in a moment when his head was clear. "You won't let them into the room to operate!"

Edgar, grim-faced and strong, stood by the bedroom door. No matter what he thought, he had given his word.

For ten days young Dwight David Eisenhower hung between life and death. His parents, deeply religious, prayed for him. They feared that the illness would mean death or, if not, would leave him crippled for life. Never again would their Dwight play the sports he loved so dearly.

Still, the decision not to amputate the leg was his alone. They refused to go against his wishes.

Somehow, almost miraculously, the fever went down. The pain disappeared. Dwight Eisenhower slowly began to get better.

Eventually he recovered. He walked again. He played football.

And he did much more.

SCHOOL
AND FAMILY

Being a child in Kansas in the 1890s (Dwight had been born on October 14, 1890) meant doing hard physical work. Dwight and his five brothers (still another brother died in infancy) had to feed the chickens, milk the family cow, and wash the clothing. For extra spending money the Eisenhower boys grew tomatoes, radishes, and carrots. Then they sold them house to house on the north side of Abilene—the section where the "rich people" lived.

Whenever Dwight wanted a baseball glove or a football helmet (his school didn't pay for such "frills") he had to earn the money. His mother had learned to make Mexican tamales in Denison, Texas, where Dwight was born. By watching her, Dwight mastered the skill. Then he turned a profit selling the tamales at

Dwight David Eisenhower's
birthplace in Denison, Texas

three for a nickel. Whatever he and his brothers could not sell, they ate.

It took Dwight's parents fourteen years before they could afford to buy a house of their own in Abilene. And even then, each of the six Eisenhower boys had to share a room and a double bed with another brother.

Dwight's father worked as an engineer, servicing the refrigeration machines in a creamery a short distance from the family's home. Years later, Dwight still remembered his father learning about the machines from a correspondence course, studying at night at the dining room table by the light of a kerosene lamp.

By the time Dwight was sixteen and a high-school student, he, too, was spending his evenings at work in the creamery. In the mornings he did his regular farm chores and his homework before setting out for school.

Today some people might think of the Eisenhowers as poor but what the Eisenhower family lacked in wealth they made up in love. David and Elizabeth Eisenhower never argued in front of their children. They showed affection for each other and the boys. They made clear exactly what they expected of their sons—what they considered right and wrong.

When a boy broke the rules punishment was swift and severe; then the matter was forgotten. Thus, whenever David Eisenhower swatted one of his children it was because, as he put it, the boy had "done a bad thing," not because he was "a bad boy."

The sons grew up to respect their parents and to love them. And the beliefs and principles of those parents

Dwight's parents, David and Ida, on their wedding day, September 23, 1885

came to shape the children's lives.

Dwight's mother especially influenced him. He later recalled his violent temper as a child. One Halloween his parents refused to let him go out trick-or-treating with his two older brothers, Arthur and Edgar. Furious, Dwight pounded his fists into an old apple tree until his hands were red with blood.

His father swatted him and sent him off to bed. Later, while he was still sobbing, his mother came to his room. For a long time she just sat in the rocking chair near his bed. Then, after he calmed down, she talked to him about the Bible's teaching that the person who conquers his soul is greater than the soldier who conquers a city. She explained how anger only hurts the person who is angry. Then she bandaged his hands and kissed him good night. Soon he fell sound asleep.

In later life, Dwight practiced an unusual way of forgetting his anger at someone. He would write the name of the person he was angry with on a piece of paper.

Then he would crumple the paper and put it in the lowest drawer of his desk. In his mind, then, the incident was over—finished—and he had no need to waste his energy on hating.

Hating, he had learned, usually was like pounding the old apple tree with his fists. The hater only hurt himself.

In school, Dwight's academic grades were only fair. What he especially enjoyed, though, were books about history's heroes. His favorites in American history were George Washington, Abraham Lincoln, and Robert E. Lee. They interested him, inspired him.

In ancient history, a subject he especially liked, his special hero was Hannibal—the Carthaginian who, against seemingly impossible odds, crossed the Alps with his elephants and nearly succeeded in destroying the mighty Roman army. It was Hannibal's courage that Dwight most admired. With defeat all but certain, Hannibal still found ways to defend his country.

Along with courage, young Dwight Eisenhower came

Dwight, from his 1909 school yearbook

to admire two other qualities—loyalty and high character. He came across those virtues not only in his reading but in his own family. For the rest of his life those were the models he used for the friends he chose, as well as for his own actions.

Dwight gave little thought to a career until 1909, the year he was to graduate from high school. Until then sports and work consumed almost all of his time. He and his brother Edgar graduated together, Edgar having lost a year to illness.

Both Dwight and Edgar Eisenhower wanted to go on to college, but clearly the family did not have enough money to send both of them. So the boys agreed early in their senior year that one brother would go on; the other would work for a year to help support the one in college. They flipped a coin to see who would first go on to school.

Edgar won. In the autumn he enrolled at the University of Michigan.

Ike took a job as night foreman at the creamery. He worked an eighty-four-hour week, supporting himself and also paying Edgar's expenses at college.

The brothers understood, of course, that by taking turns going to school they could not finish for many years. As a result, Ike decided to try a shortcut.

In September 1910, he wrote to Senator Joseph Bristow of Kansas, asking for an appointment either to the U.S. Naval Academy at Annapolis or to the U.S. Military Academy at West Point.

Senator Bristow responded to Ike that appointments

To earn money for a college education, Dwight worked 12-hour days at the Abilene Creamery.

would not simply be handed out, as usual. Instead, there would be an examination in October.

October! That meant young Eisenhower had only one month to prepare while still working his eighty-four-hour-a-week schedule at the creamery.

For the next month Ike crammed for the test, taking study time from the few hours he had set aside for sleep.

He placed first in the state on the exam for Annapolis, second for West Point.

Ike preferred Annapolis. But because he had lost so much time by working and by repeating a school year after his bout with blood poisoning, he was too old for the Naval Academy. Meanwhile, the student who had won first place on the West Point exam failed his army physical.

Senator Bristow offered the U.S. Military Academy appointment to Dwight Eisenhower. He accepted it.

In June 1911, carrying one battered old suitcase filled with hand-me-down clothing from his brother, Ike said good-bye to his family and to Abilene.

On a sweltering summer day Dwight Eisenhower arrived at the railroad station in West Point, New York. From there, along with many of the other new cadets, he made the long, winding uphill climb to the famous plain overlooking the Hudson River.

At the top, gazing out over the plain, he caught his first glimpse of the Gothic building of the U.S. Military Academy.

WEST POINT

Ike fit easily into the West Point pattern. Older, and more confident than other cadets, he took with a smile the hazing that upperclassmen gave to plebes—first-year students. To him it was just a test: could a plebe stand pressure, take orders, not get rattled? Those qualities, he knew, were necessary in an army officer.

Pictures of Cadet Dwight D. Eisenhower reveal the same kind of person his friends and neighbors knew in Abilene—calm, sensible, ambitious, but also watchful and a little bit wary.

Almost from the beginning Ike played varsity football for the Academy, winning praise from a New York newspaper as "one of the most promising backs in the East." Then, in 1912, during his sophomore year, a knee injury

in the Tufts game abruptly ended his dream of glory in sports. Until then he had even toyed with the idea of becoming a professional athlete after college.

Discouraged, Ike's grades dropped. As he later remembered, "Life seemed to have little meaning."

But he never stayed discouraged for long. When he was given a chance to coach the junior varsity football squad, his enthusiasm returned. Senior officers at West Point, observing the way he handled his coaching duties, labeled him "a man born to command."

In 1915 he graduated from West Point. In the class of 164 cadets he placed a respectable 61st in academic standing. Yet, because he was always casual about such matters as polishing his brass buttons and being on time for meals, he ranked 125th in conduct, with an astonishing 211 demerits.

Dwight David Eisenhower's West Point graduation portrait, June 15, 1915

MARRIAGE, WAR, AND TRAGEDY

Ike graduated from West Point as a second lieutenant. His first duty assignment was Fort Sam Houston, Texas. There he was introduced to a saucy, pretty girl of eighteen named Mamie Geneva Doud.

Before meeting Mamie, Ike had shown little interest in girls. Yet on Valentine's Day 1916, only four months after meeting her, he offered Mamie Doud an engagement ring. In July they were married, Mamie wearing a bridal gown of white lace, Ike his formal dress-white uniform.

From the beginning Mamie proved to be a good choice as an army wife. She accepted with good humor, even laughter, the cramped quarters they had to live in at Fort Sam Houston. She learned the unwritten but strict social rules that officers' wives had to live by.

Mamie and Dwight were married
in Denver on July 1, 1916.

In 1917, Mamie gave birth to a son, Doud Dwight Eisenhower, or as she and Ike liked to call him, "Little Icky."

In the spring of that same year President Woodrow Wilson asked Congress for a declaration of war against Germany. Ike tried frantically to get to the scene of battle in Europe. Again and again, however, his superiors turned down his pleas. He was so successful as a trainer of new recruits that they would not let him go. Swiftly, he rose to the rank of lieutenant colonel.

His orders finally came through to sail to France. But before he could sail, World War I had ended.

With peace came an economy drive. Congress cut the army to the bare bone. Ike was reduced in rank to captain. The future seemed without promise. He seriously considered leaving his military career altogether.

Just then a stunning blow struck Ike and Mamie: in January 1921 "Little Icky" died of scarlet fever. It was, Eisenhower said many years later, "the greatest disappointment and disaster in my life, the one I have never been able to forget completely."

This family picture of Mamie, "Icky," and Dwight was taken in 1918. The death of their first son was a blow from which Dwight never quite recovered.

THE ARMY'S INNER CIRCLE

Just when things looked darkest for him, there came a ray of light. While stationed at Fort Meade, Maryland, he had come to know a number of tank officers. He became especially close with one of them, a colorful, tough colonel named George S. Patton.

In World War I, the tank had been used mostly as support for infantry. But Eisenhower and Patton saw it as a devastating weapon, one that possibly could play a decisive role if used in daring attacks in mass numbers. Together they wrote articles about tank warfare that appeared in military magazines.

But that was not the message their superiors wanted to hear. Eisenhower and Patton, ahead of their time, were ordered to stop writing their articles or be court-martialed and dismissed from the army. Another officer, Billy Mitchell, had a similar experience—he actually *was* court-martialed when he insisted on describing the future uses of bombing planes.

In the case of Eisenhower and Patton, one influential officer, Brig. Gen. Fox Conner, took up their cause. Conner came to see in young Eisenhower the qualities of future military greatness. He described Ike as "a man of force, character, and energy, as well as knowledge."

In 1922, General Conner arranged to have Eisenhower transferred to his command staff in the Panama Canal Zone. It was Conner's belief that a second world war was certain. When that war began, he said, Ike should be prepared to lead; the country would need him.

Brigadier General Fox Conner

For three years Conner taught Eisenhower everything he knew. He gave him lessons on the importance of international trade, raw materials, and national interests and how they all related to military strategy. He encouraged Ike's interest in military history and had him study about great commanders and battles of the past. He set up make-believe battle situations and had Eisenhower plan strategies for winning.

At last, Conner thought his pupil was ready. In 1926, he arranged for Ike's assignment to the army's Command and General Staff School at Fort Leavenworth, Kansas. At that school the U.S. Army decides which officers will become its real leaders, its commanding generals. The academic program is so demanding that many officers drop out, some from fatigue, others for lack of mental ability.

In his class of 275 officers Dwight David Eisenhower ranked at the very top.

One of his officers there was Col. George S. Patton, his old friend. "Someday, Eisenhower, I'll be working for you," said Patton.

"How's that for a laugh!" declared the modest Ike, reporting the story to Mamie.

In 1927, Eisenhower was sent to the Army War College in Washington, D.C., a goal sought by every army officer. Again he graduated first in his class. Clearly now he was being watched by his superiors—marked as a man on his way up.

Meanwhile, in 1922, Mamie had given birth to anoth-

This segment of a group photo of the Command and General Staff School at Fort Leavenworth, Kansas, was of the 1925–26 class. Eisenhower can be seen in the second row from the top, third from the left.

Eisenhower displayed his keen ability to do his job under very difficult circumstance in the Philippines. Here he is shown with other U.S. military officers at the Malacanang Palace in Manila: Tex Lee (left), Douglas MacArthur (center), and Eisenhower (right).

er son, John. Remembering what had happened to their first child, Ike and Mamie lavished affection on him.

In 1928, Eisenhower was sent to Europe to write a guidebook to the battlefields where American soldiers had fought in World War I. His book won the praise of an American hero of that war, Gen. John J. Pershing.

The book also led to Ike's appointment in 1932 to the War Department in Washington. It was there that he met Gen. Douglas MacArthur, the army chief of staff and a man destined to be one of the outstanding figures in American military history.

MacArthur immediately admired Eisenhower's intelligence, his ability to get quickly to the very heart of a problem. He also liked Ike's total honesty and his habit of reporting the facts as they were, not as he wanted them to be.

In 1933, MacArthur made Ike his personal assistant. Two years later, when MacArthur became military adviser to the Philippine government, he ordered Ike to go along with him to the Far East. Reluctantly, Eisenhower agreed.

In the Philippines, Eisenhower had to deal with the country's highest leaders. Many of them did not want the Americans there at all. They wanted to run their own affairs without the help of the United States. Yet even many of those officers came to respect Ike. Friendly, natural—completely himself—he won them over. In 1940, when the time came for Eisenhower to leave the Philippines, that country's president offered him a blank check—he could fill in any salary he wanted to stay on as his adviser. Graciously, Eisenhower refused.

A HERO OF WORLD WAR II

On September 1, 1939, Adolf Hitler sent his German armies crashing into Poland. England and France answered with a declaration of war. Just as Fox Conner had predicted, a second world war had broken out.

In the summer of 1940 Dwight Eisenhower, by then a colonel, took charge of the Third Army's maneuvers (war games) in Louisiana. He had to work mostly with raw recruits, men drafted right out of civilian life. Ike's "Blue Army" won the games.

On December 7, 1941, the Japanese launched a surprise attack on the American naval base at Pearl Harbor, Hawaii.

Five days later Gen. George C. Marshall, then the army chief of staff, sent urgent orders to Eisenhower to

As Supreme Allied Commander, General Eisenhower (first row, center) directed the activities of these eleven commanding officers (front row from left): Lt. Gen. William H. Simpson, Gen. George S. Patton, Jr., Gen. Carl A. Speatz, Gen. Omar N. Bradley, Gen. Courtney H. Hodges, Lt. Gen. Leonard T. Gerow; (back row, from left): Brig. Gen. Ralph F. Stearley, Lt. Gen Hoyt S. Vandenberg, Lt. Gen. Walter B. Smith, Otto P. Watland, Brig. Gen. Richard E. Nugent.

join his staff in Washington at once. His job: to direct the total planning of America's early strategy in the war against Japan.

In choosing Eisenhower, Marshall jumped over hundreds of officers who were ahead of him in rank and in length of service. Marshall, it turned out, had been watching Ike's development for years, waiting for just the right moment to use his talents.

Swiftly, Eisenhower chose a team of the most capable men in the army, including some of his West Point classmates. Before long General Marshall promoted him to assistant chief of staff in charge of war plans. Ike's biggest new task was to draw up an overall plan for the rest of the war in Europe—a plan that would defeat the Germans and end the fighting.

Marshall questioned Ike's plan closely, testing it for weakness just as the Germans would. Then he accepted it—exactly as written. Marshall went one step further. He appointed Eisenhower commanding general, European Theater of Operations. Ike would have a chance to carry out his own plan.

By then a lieutenant general (three stars), Eisenhower organized an American attack on North Africa in 1942 to relieve some of the pressure on the British forces fighting there. After the Germans had been chased out of Africa, he next helped plan the 1943 Allied landings in Sicily and Italy.

Finally the time came for the most important, most dangerous move in the war: an invasion of France from

**Gen. Eisenhower in Tunisia,
North Africa, in 1943**

across the English Channel and, from there, a thrust into the heart of Germany.

In December 1943, President Franklin D. Roosevelt, with the agreement of Prime Minister Winston Churchill of England, chose Dwight Eisenhower as supreme commander of all the Allied forces.

On June 6, 1944, Ike launched the grandest invasion in all of human history, smashing into the beaches of Normandy on the coast of France. His force included more than a million men, eleven thousand planes, four thousand ships.

Waiting for them on the beaches were tough, experienced German troops and a bristling chain of fortifications designed by the finest minds in the German army.

On the day of the attack—known as "D-Day"—it appeared for a time that the Germans would overwhelm the Allied force and drive the invaders back into the sea. The deciding factor was the high morale and the courage of the ordinary Allied soldier, fighting sometimes in hand-to-hand combat.

Eisenhower himself had played a special part in building that morale, that courage.

Despite heavy losses, the Allied beachhead held firm.

Then, in the weeks that followed, the Allies finally

Eisenhower and his staff examine the results of the Nazi atrocities at the German concentration camp at Gotha, Germany.

stormed out of their positions on the beach and raced across France.

They liberated Paris.

They swarmed across the Rhine and thundered on toward Berlin.

On the way, they stumbled onto the death camps, where Hitler's henchmen had tortured and killed millions of victims. Ike, visiting one of the camps, stared in disgust and disbelief at the horror of it.

On April 30, 1945, Hitler committed suicide. One week later, in a redbrick schoolhouse on the outskirts of Reims, France, the Germans surrendered.

After signing the surrender document, the German commander, Alfred Jodl, was taken to General Eisenhower's headquarters. Ike knew what the Germans had stood for; he had seen the death camps. Curtly, he asked Jodl if he understood what he had signed, and then warned him that he was personally responsible for living up to the terms.

"That is all," snapped Eisenhower, dismissing the German without returning his salute.

In August 1945, American planes dropped atomic bombs on two Japanese cities, Hiroshima and Nagasaki. Japan surrendered.

World War II at last was over.

Gen. Gustaf Jodl signs Germany's unconditional surrender on May 6, 1945, ending the war in Europe.

FROM PRESIDENT OF A COLLEGE TO PRESIDENT OF THE NATION

For a time Ike stayed on in Europe to organize the Allied occupation of Germany. Then, with General Marshall's retirement, he became army chief of staff. By that time he wore on his uniform five stars, the highest rank in the American military.

Everywhere he was greeted as a hero. New York City arranged a ticker-tape parade for him. Major corporations offered him incredible salaries to serve as their president.

Meanwhile, politicians pleaded with him to run for office.

Instead, in October 1948, he became president of Columbia University, in New York City.

Although Eisenhower was not an academic, he knew how to choose good advisers and get the most out of them. He guided Columbia through a time of major problems, both academic and financial.

General Dwight David Eisenhower returns to the United States a hero. New York City greets the general with a massive ticker-tape parade on June 19, 1945.

Then, unexpectedly, Ike found himself back in uniform. At the end of World War II the United States had largely disarmed and disbanded its army, but the Soviet Union had not. In place after place, the Soviets tested the will of their former allies. Finally, in June 1950, North Korean troops armed by the Soviets invaded South Korea.

A few months later President Harry Truman telephoned Eisenhower. A new alliance, the North Atlantic Treaty Organization (NATO), was being formed to unite the defense forces of Western Europe. Would Ike agree to be the NATO supreme commander?

Ever since childhood Dwight Eisenhower had been trained to do his duty, to accept responsibility. It was a quality he always had admired in his heroes from history, such as George Washington. To leave his pleasant life as president of Columbia would not be easy. It would be a sacrifice.

Ike agreed at once to serve his country.

Other generals could have organized NATO. Possibly they could have done the job just as efficiently. The difference was that Eisenhower brought to the job a sense of purpose, of high idealism, and of faith.

As supreme commander of NATO in 1951–1952,

President Harry S. Truman asked Gen. Eisenhower to return to the military in June 1950 to be Supreme Commander of the newly formed North Atlantic Treaty Organization (NATO).

Dwight Eisenhower gave spine and toughness and confidence to the leaders of the free world. He inspired them to action.

* * *

As the presidential election of 1952 approached, it became impossible for Dwight Eisenhower to stay out of American politics. Time after time he had denied interest in becoming a presidential candidate. At last, however, he gave in.

America needed his leadership. It was his duty to serve. And, for Ike, it was impossible not to take on responsibility.

At the Republican National Convention in cheers rang out wildly across the convention hall:

"I like Ike!"

"I like Ike!"

"I like Ike!"

Eisenhower won the Republican nomination. In the November election he swept to victory over the Democratic candidate, the witty, eloquent governor of Illinois, Adlai E. Stevenson.

In 1956 he defeated Stevenson by an even broader margin and went on to serve a second four-year term as president.

President and Mrs. Dwight David
Eisenhower during his first term
inaugural ceremonies on January 20, 1953.

YEARS IN THE WHITE HOUSE

Dwight Eisenhower's eight years in the White House were filled with dramatic events. In foreign affairs he accomplished many things:

• Succeeded in ending the Korean War by negotiating a compromise truce settlement with the Soviet Union following the death of the Soviet leader, Joseph Stalin. Korea, however, remained divided between the Communist North and the democratic South.

• Sent military and economic aid to the Middle East to end the conflict between Egypt, which had seized the Suez Canal, and the three countries—Israel, Great Britain, and France—that had joined together to punish the Egyptians.

• Strengthened NATO, primarily through the Eisenhower Doctrine, which promised that American forces could be used to help any nation threatened by international communism.

- Organized the Southeast Asia Treaty Organization (SEATO) to prevent the further spread of communism in Indochina and to check the expansion of China.

- Suggested to Soviet Premier Nikita S. Khrushchev the Atoms for Peace program, which he hoped would bring nuclear cooperation between the two superpowers.

- Proposed to Khrushchev the dramatic Open Skies plan, which allowed the United States and the Soviet Union to freely survey each other's territories and military activities. This arrangement later collapsed.

- Reacted sharply to Fidel Castro's rise to power in 1959 as Communist dictator of Cuba. Eisenhower broke off diplomatic relations with Cuba and declared an embargo on any further U.S. trade with that country. He also announced that the United States would use force if necessary to stop the spread of Communist dictatorships to other nations in Latin America.

In domestic affairs, too, President Eisenhower acted with great strength. He:

- Dispatched U.S. troops to Little Rock, Arkansas, to uphold the Supreme Court's order calling for racial desegregation of schools. Eisenhower had appointed Earl Warren to the position of chief justice of the U.S. Supreme Court, which, under Warren, ruled segregation unconstitutional.

- Supported the Civil Rights Acts of 1957 and 1960, intended to protect the voting rights of people, regardless of their race, color, or religion.

Premier Nikita Khrushchev visits with President Eisenhower at Camp David, the presidential retreat in Maryland.

What an eventful, dramatic eight-year period, one filled with achievement and accomplishment!

For a time it was popular for historians to look down on Eisenhower's presidency—to say that he gave America too little direction. One historian called him "Dwight the Dull" and described his administration as "a time of drift."

But the tide of historical judgment has turned. Many historians now consider him among America's finest presidents. According to one prominent scholar, Eisenhower soon will be ranked with Woodrow Wilson, Theodore Roosevelt, and Franklin Roosevelt as one of the four truly great presidents of the twentieth century.

With time, Ike's qualities as a person have come to stand out more clearly. It was no accident, for example, that Gen. George C. Marshall, perhaps the greatest military mind in America's history, chose Ike over so many other senior officers to be commanding general in Europe.

He knew Eisenhower as a man of intelligence, drive, ambition, and even ruthlessness. And Marshall was aware that Ike had disciplined his emotions and learned to make hard decisions, even when they involved great risk. If, for example, Eisenhower had postponed the D-Day attack one month because of bad weather, as some of his aides suggested, Soviet troops might well have overrun all of Western Europe.

As president, Ike sometimes appeared to speak in riddles. Although he was never as good a speaker as he was a writer, much of his apparent confusion was inten-

Dwight and Mamie celebrated their thirty-ninth wedding anniversary with a large lawn buffet supper for the White House staff in 1955.

tional. Before one press conference, an aide expressed his fear that reporters would ask embarrassing questions on a certain issue. "Don't worry," Ike told him. "If it comes up, I'll confuse them."

So as not to look too smart to average Americans, he sometimes cut out excellent phrases from his speeches. Similarly, he claimed to reporters that he read only mystery stories and westerns, when actually he continued to be a serious student of history.

Behind Ike's broad, boyish grin stood a tough politician. To Premier Khrushchev he spoke of Atoms for Peace, but he let his secretary of state, John Foster Dulles, speak freely of massive retaliation—striking back at Soviet political moves with atomic bombs.

Eisenhower also was a realist. Although a military man, he turned down the advice of most of his generals in 1954 about going to war in Vietnam. To Ike, that seemed like a great risk for a small gain—not good odds for an old poker player. He also cut spending for expensive new weapons, saying that most of them would be outdated before they were ready for use.

America, said President Eisenhower, needed a time of "serenity and confidence." He wanted to unite the country and make the economy strong. After the bitter conflicts among races and social classes, rich and poor, that had marked the 1930s and 1940s, he tried to bring people together. His goals were economic growth and stability. Perhaps that is why Americans today often look back on his years in office, the 1950s, with a certain longing.

RETIREMENT AND DEATH

Dwight Eisenhower retired in 1961, and John F. Kennedy became president of the United States. Ike and Mamie bought a farm at Gettysburg, Pennsylvania, near the Civil War battlefield there. Often they traveled to Europe, meeting with people Ike had known during the war.

At home he painted, even exhibiting and selling some of his works. He wrote books about his youth in Kansas and about his wartime experiences. He also enjoyed playing golf.

Visitors, including some of the world's best-known people, flocked to Gettysburg. Eisenhower greeted them with warmth and friendship.

One of his political foes, the Senate majority leader, Lyndon Baines Johnson, summed up his feelings for

The former president and his first lady retire to their beloved home in Gettysburg, Pennsylvania.

Eisenhower simply, saying "I like him." Later, as president, Johnson often called Ike to the White House for advice.

During his own presidency Ike suffered two massive heart attacks, each time causing the stock market to drop sharply because of business's high confidence in him.

He recovered from those illnesses. At last, however, his health gave out completely. One heart attack followed another.

On March 28, 1969, after a gallant fight for life at the Walter Reed Army Medical Center in Washington, Dwight D. Eisenhower died.

According to his wishes, his body was returned to Abilene for burial not far from his boyhood home.

* * *

Speaking once in London, shortly after Germany's surrender in 1945, Ike remarked that Denison, Texas, where he was born, and Abilene, Kansas, where he grew up, were not equal in population to one five hundredth of London. Those American towns, he said, were young by British standards, without the ancient traditions of British cities. Still, said Eisenhower, he was proud of his people. He continued:

> A Londoner will fight to preserve his freedom of worship, his equality before the law, his liberty to speak and act as he sees fit. . . . So will a citizen of Abilene.
>
> When we consider these things, then the valley of the Thames [the river running through London] draws closer to the farms of Kansas and the plains of Texas.

**President Eisenhower greatly enjoyed
the relaxation he received from painting.**

Dwight David Eisenhower sprang from the heartland
of America. Like Abraham Lincoln, he was one of the people. He belonged to them. And he never forgot that.

CONCLUSION: THE MEANING OF A LIFE

Ike is often pictured grinning broadly—his arms thrust skyward, his fingers in a "V" to celebrate the victory of his troops, the American GIs and their Allied comrades, in World War II.

We see him later as one of the presidents who, early in the Cold War, marshaled the strength of the free world against the Soviet menace.

Yet, like so many leaders who are characteristically American, Dwight Eisenhower had to grapple with—and to triumph over—challenges that would have defeated a lesser human being.

He first had to go beyond his origins as an obscure farm boy and his struggle with an injury that could have left him crippled.

He then lived an adult life cut to the American mold.

From the beginning, when the pioneers first set out to conquer the wilderness, Americans have been at the same time dreamers and people of practical affairs. One writer has described them as "idealists working in matter." Throughout his career Eisenhower was eager for success, but he also had what President Woodrow Wilson called "a passion for the rights of man."

Ike's dream—"the promise of American life"—has never faded. And now, at the end of the twentieth century, a generation of new immigrants, drawn from Latin America and Asia, is finding a safe haven and new opportunity here. "This America is an ancient land," declared the writer Edgar Lee Masters, "forever new to hands that keep it new."

Always it has been the real hands of real people that have shaped our national past, and those hands will continue to shape our future. And that same faith—the belief that individuals can make a difference in their own lives and in the life of their country—is still with us.

That belief was a touchstone in the life of the uniquely American personality whose story you have read—Dwight David Eisenhower.

IMPORTANT DATES

October 14, 1890	Dwight David Eisenhower is born in Denison, Texas.
1911	Chosen for admission to West Point.
1916	Marries Mamie Geneva Doud.
1926	Graduates first in his class at Command and General Staff School.
1928	Graduates first in his class at Army War College.
1933–1939	Serves under General Douglas MacArthur in Washington and in the Philippines.
December 7, 1941	Japanese attack Pearl Harbor, bringing United States into World War II.
June 1942	Becomes commander of U.S. forces in Europe.
July 1942	Named Allied commander in chief for invasion of North Africa.
1943	Leads invasions of Sicily and Italy.
December 1943	Becomes commander in chief of Allied forces preparing for invasion of Europe.
June 6, 1944	D-Day landing of Allied forces in France.
1944	Becomes five-star general.
May 8, 1945	Accepts Germany's surrender at Reims, France.
1945	Commands U.S. occupation forces in Germany.
1948	Becomes president of Columbia University and publishes *Crusade in Europe.*
1950	Named commander of NATO forces.
1952	Elected president of the United States.
1956	Reelected to the presidency.
1963	Publishes his memoirs, *Mandate for Change.*
March 28, 1969	Dwight David Eisenhower dies.

FOR FURTHER READING

The two leading biographies of Dwight D. Eisenhower are *Eisenhower* by Stephen E. Ambrose (1983) and *Eisenhower: Portrait of the Hero* by Peter Lyon (1973). No work however, gives clearer insight into Ike's values—the ideals he stood for—than his own book, *Crusade in Europe* (1948).

Books for Young Readers

Carpenter, Allan. *Dwight David Eisenhower: The Warring Peacemaker*. Vero Beach, Fla.: Rourke Publications, 1987.

Darby, Jean. *Dwight D. Eisenhower: A Man Called Ike*. Minneapolis: Lerner Publications, 1989.

Ellis, Rafaela. *Dwight D. Eisenhower: 34th President of*

the United States. Ada, Okla.: Garrett Educational Corp., 1989.

Hargrove, Jim. *Dwight D. Eisenhower: Thirty-Fourth President of the United States*. Chicago: Childrens Press, 1987.

Sandberg, Peter Lars. *Dwight D. Eisenhower*. New York: Chelsea House, 1986.

Van Steenwyk, Elizabeth. *Dwight David Eisenhower, President*. New York: Walker, 1987.

Wilkinson, Philip. *Generals Who Changed the World*. New York: Chelsea House, 1994.

INDEX

ABOUT THE AUTHOR

William Jay Jacobs has studied history at Harvard, Yale, and Princeton and holds a doctorate from Columbia. He has held fellowships with the Ford Foundation and the National Endowment for the Humanities and served as a Fulbright Fellow in India. In addition to broad teaching experience in public and private secondary schools, he has taught at Rutgers University, at Hunter College, and at Harvard. Dr. Jacobs presently is Visiting Fellow in History at Yale.

Among his previous books for young readers are biographies of such diverse personalities as Abraham Lincoln, Eleanor Roosevelt, Edgar Allan Poe, Hannibal, Hitler, and Mother Teresa. His *America's Story* and *History of the United States* are among the nation's most widely used textbooks.

In the Franklin Watts First Book series, he is the author of *Magellan, Cortés, Pizarro, La Salle, Champlain,* and *Coronado.*